FIRST TIME HOME BUYING BASICS

Josh Mattison

Copyright © 2021 Josh Mattison

All rights reserved

The characters and events portrayed in this book are fictitious. Any similarity to real persons, living or dead, is coincidental and not intended by the author.

No part of this book may be reproduced, or stored in a retrieval system, or transmitted in any form or by any means, electronic, mechanical, photocopying, recording, or otherwise, without express written permission of the publisher.

ISBN-13: 9798739942906
ISBN-10: 1477123456

Cover design by: Josh Mattison
Library of Congress Control Number: 2018675309
Printed in the United States of America

I want to give a special thanks to my wonderfully loving parents, Greg and Diane Mattison. They started our family owned real estate company when I was just a kid in school. They have been self-employed, as far back as I can remember, and have always valued independence. My parents taught me how to work for myself, use my mind, and use my talents to create my own path in life. None of this would be possible if I didn't have their love and support.

I also want to thank my loving partner Emma Paunil for encouraging me to write this book in the first place. Emma believes in me and continues to help me live life as my highest self.

CONTENTS

Title Page
Copyright
Dedication
Introduction
Chapter 1: Where do I start?   1
Chapter 2: How much can I comfortably afford?   9
Chapter 3: Loans   21
Chapter 4: Understanding interest rates.   32
Chapter 5: Closing Costs   45
Chapter 6: The Purchase Process   52
Chapter 7: Closing the Deal   68
Afterword   85
About The Author   87
First Time Home Buying Basics   89

INTRODUCTION

Welcome to First Time Home Buying Basics. I'm Josh Mattison a residential real estate broker in the state of Arizona, and have helped 100's of buyers and sellers through a successful sales process over the years. Everyone has to be a first time buyer or seller at some point when it comes to home ownership. It can seem a little intimidating and possibly stressful when it comes to all the paperwork and legalities. Bank financing, purchase contracts, and closing documents can seem like an ocean of endless paperwork and monetary jargon. An ever changing cyclical real estate market full of booms and busts can make your head spin. Somehow every first time buyer needs to navigate their way through all of this to decide what's the best move for them to make.

That's why I decided to write this book. I wanted to create a guide in not only the technical sales process. I wanted to address the practical real life issues and thought process of helping you as a buyer decide what's best for you. I've arranged each chapter in chronological order leading you through the purchase process, just as I personally have done for the clients I've helped over the years. We will start by getting into the right mindset by addressing some of the most common questions and concerns buyers come across. We'll start with basic thought provoking questions like, why do I need to buy a home? What kind of real estate market are we currently in? What can I afford? Is bank financing my only option? By getting a clear answer on these basic questions will naturally lead us to more logical questions. What's the difference between a down payment and closing costs? Why do I need to care about what my interest rate is? Yay I have an accepted contract on the house...now what happens? Throughout this book I will break down the complex financial and real estate jargon into simple terms and easy steps to follow.

By the end of this book you will know exactly what steps to take down the path of homeownership.

CHAPTER 1: WHERE DO I START?

Where do I start? Well that's a good question. Let's look at what brought you to that question in the first place. Somehow or some way you found yourself interested in the idea of buying a home. Maybe someone you know just bought a home, and invited you over to show and tell you all about it. There are countless ways you could have come up with the idea of, "hey maybe I should buy a home". Whatever that idea is, has just become your "why". Over the years I have worked as a residential real estate broker, I would meet new, soon-to-be-buyers and they would say to me:

"I want to buy a home!"

My response would be, "Fantastic! What's your why?"

After the puzzled look and awkward silence was more than

we could stand, I would elaborate upon my question asking, "Why do you *need* to buy a home?" They would insert their answer, or many answers, after stumbling through reasons for a bit, and we would go from there.

What's Your Why?

Now I ask you. *What's your why?* As a new buyer this is the first most important question you need to be able to answer in the most matter-of-fact way. Most of the time I will hear people say:

"Well, because I'm sick of being a renter."

"Well why is that?" I would ask.

"Well, because I'm sick of throwing money away every month for a place I will never own. I'm just making the landlord rich, and have nothing to show for it."

"Ah," I would say, "now we're getting somewhere."

I would then remind the potential buyer that being a renter also has some benefits a homeowner does not have. For example, if your A/C or furnace breaks, you just call the landlord or the management company to come fix it. They have to pay to repair or replace that home function they promised to you as part of the rental agreement. For example, I just had the A/C completely die at my house during the summertime here in Arizona. As a homeowner, I had to pay to have it fixed. Not only that, but it was not repairable and had to be replaced. I had to come up with $5,300 on the spot for a new A/C unit, and that number was *cheap* compared to the other bids closer to the $10,000 range. This can be the case for any major repair: from the foundation of the home, all the way to the roof. If the prospective buyer accepts those risks, because they are determined to be a homeowner no matter what, then we have established a strong "why."

The other common response I would hear from prospective buyers when I asked *what's your why*, is this:

"Well, it's the American dream to own your own home."

To that I would jokingly respond with, "whose dream are we referring to?"

If you have enough money to buy your house for cash as a new homeowner, then I can possibly agree with that statement from an independence standpoint. For most of us who have been first time home buyers, or home buyers in general, you don't have that amount of cash on hand to buy one of the biggest financial purchases most people will ever make. If you don't have the cash, then you most likely will need to get a home loan from the bank. Loans come with paying interest, and paying interest over the life of the loan usually means you end up paying double the original house price you originally agreed to. We will break down bank financing and interest rates so you can see exactly what I'm talking about in a later chapter. For now think of it this way: if it's the American dream for every person to own their own home, yet you need a bank loan that will end up costing you *double* the price when you add up the interest in the end, then whose dream is it? The home buyer, or the bank? I know that might not sound very compassionate or maybe even a little harsh, but these are the questions and thoughts you must navigate as you start this journey. This will help you have a clear matter-of-fact answer to *what's your why*, and help fuel your fire to deal with any hurdles you will encounter along the way. I highly recommend that you write down the answer to *what's your why*, and the answer to this next logical question.

What Kind Of Market Are We In?

What kind of real estate market/economy are we in right now? As a new buyer, you most likely won't have a clue to what that answer is, and for the moment that's okay.

You might be saying to yourself, "Why would I need to care about what the market is right now, or our economy? That's boring stuff my grandpa listens to on the news and tries to bring up at the dinner table at family get togethers!"

Once again, not to be harsh, but once you are born into this world and its monetary system, you're officially in the economy... whether you like it or not! Child care, taxes for public schools, and student loans are all major players in the economy. Once you have a job, you are now a tax paying member of that economy as well.

You might be saying, "Ok fine, I get the point I'm part of the 'economy.' Why do I need to know what kind of real estate market/economy we are currently in?"

Well, think of it this way. Imagine you want to buy a certain computer you've been looking at, but it's kind of expensive. You like it, and really want it, so you've been saving your money. As you are getting close to being able to buy it, you find out the price is going to drop in half by next month. After all that saving and shopping, would you be willing to wait another month to get it at half price? What if you bought it now, and then found out the next month your friend bought the same computer for half the price? Wouldn't you think, "Aw man, I wish I would have known that was going to happen. I could have bought that same computer, *and* a couple new outfits for that price. Oh well, how was I supposed to know, I guess?"

Let me tell you, when it comes to the biggest purchase of your life, you should probably do your homework. This is usually when people tell me, "Hey that's why I have a realtor right? The realtor is supposed to know all that stuff, so I don't have to worry about it." As a licensed real estate broker since 2005, I say yes and no to that one. Yes, your realtor should know what the current market trends are doing. Are we in an up swing or down, or is everything just kind of going sideways at the moment? Just like the stock market, precious metals, and crypto currencies, the real estate market moves in a cyclical manner. It has many ups and downs; booms and busts. Your realtor should have a general gauge on where the market seems to be.

Not to bash any of my fellow realtors, but please keep in mind... realtors get paid by commission. If you buy a house, they get paid; if you don't, they don't. If you tell them you want to buy a house right now no matter what, because you are sick of wasting money paying rent, you can bet your assets they are going to help you do what you want! You are, what we call in the business, a very "motivated buyer." It's now in your, and your realtor's, best interest to find you a home, just like you asked for. At this point, doing any research on what kind of market we're in is going to be assumed that you've already done that. If you don't have the "what kind of market are we in" discussion with your realtor first, don't assume your realtor is going to automatically have it with you.

That's why I recommend *you* educate yourself first, at least right now at this point. Spend some quality time with grandpa watching the news and talking about it. Don't stop there though, as the news is filtered by the companies that own the channels. Get on YouTube and watch as many different videos as you can find by real estate investors and gurus. See what they are saying about the current market we are in, and where it seems to be heading towards. The average person lives in their home 5 to 7 years before moving. Having some insight on where the market is going might make a difference to you. In one night of watching videos by real estate professionals, you will have plenty of information to start forming your own opinion. Heck, you might have some ammo to throw back at grandpa that his news channels aren't telling him! The better financial education you expose yourself to, the better chance you give yourself for informed decisions. Depending on what you find out and come up with, you might even end up changing your answer to, *what's your why*. Even if the answer is to hold off and wait for that new computer price to drop, that's okay. Now you have a plan, and possibly some extra cash in your pocket, by thinking and questioning your way to success. Speaking of cash, let's talk about that in the next chapter as we discover your possible hidden purchase powers!

CHAPTER 2: HOW MUCH CAN I COMFORTABLY AFFORD?

Assuming you know the answer to the first two questions from Chapter 1, *What's your why*, and *what kind of real estate market are we in?*, let's explore the next logical question: *How much can you, "comfortably", afford?* I say, "comfortably", because you want to stay within your means. You want to be able to enjoy your life, by having time to do all the things you want to do, right? If you want to avoid being a wage-slave, working long hours to pay for a home you barely spend any time in, because you are always working at your job to pay for this house you can't afford, then this is your chance right now to find out what you can *comfortably afford*.

Let's use the following questions to discover your purchase powers. Writing your answers down will help develop a guide for you to follow should you pursue your home buying conquest. If you're anything like me, you're not going to stop reading and go get a piece of paper right now to answer these questions. Don't worry, I got your back, and listed the questions here in the book for you to fill out. You just have to meet me halfway by getting something to write with. Maybe if you're really like me, you can holler for someone to bring you a pencil or pen. If not, then show the law of action how motivated you are, by getting up and finding something to write with now. I'll wait,... oh and grab me something to drink while you're up, thanks!

Awesome, welcome back, and thanks for the drink. Cheers to you for taking action, and for taking a step in the direction of making the home buying thought a reality. When you write things down, they instantly go from nothing, to something. They start to become real right before your very eyes. Since we're getting kind of personal, let me ask you a question: Where are you living right now, and how much do you currently pay per month? You will see this is one of your questions to answer on your list, right under the other two questions I snuck in there from the last chapter. I didn't know how serious you were taking this whole home buying mission thing, but now that you're on Chapter 2, things just got real. Okay, now that you have your monthly expenses in mind, let me ask you another question. Can you afford all of your bills and living expenses fairly easily? If so, how much cash are you able to save per month? Do you have enough saved to be able to buy a house for cash? If you are a first time buyer, most likely the answer is no, and that's ok. We have a few other avenues to explore for discovering more purchase powers.

Toys

Do you have any cool toys I can play with? I'm not talking about dolls, or action figures... I mean expensive toys I can break that cost lots of money to fix! Things like off road vehicles, boats, jet skis, extra vehicles, and travel trailers. If so, how much do you actually use them? Do you owe money on them still, or are you making payments? If so, how much is your payment? If you didn't have that payment, how much could you be saving to buy your house? How much could you sell any of those toys for right now? If you have any of these cool toys, you're probably saying, "No way man, I'm not selling those." Hey I don't blame you, plus the name of this game is to enjoy your life with what you can comfortably afford. If you have to sell all your fun things you enjoy just to max yourself out to buy a home, then what's the fun in that? At the same time, if buying a home is now more important to you than toys sitting around that you don't use, then maybe this is something you should be considering. Worse yet is if you not only *don't* use these toys, but you *still* owe money on them or are making monthly payments. Worst of all the situations would be: you *don't* use them, you're still paying them off, *and* you are paying to have them stored somewhere. That's like a triple whammy! The point is, these are items you can use to free up some cash, and save yourself some money, if your priorities change on what's important to you.

Investments

Let's get even more personal. Do you have any investments you can tell me about? Besides savings accounts, do you have stocks, silver, gold, crypto currencies? What about a college fund put away for you, that you've never used? Maybe some inheritance money kept safely away from you, so you wouldn't blow it on those toys you got? I know of people who have parents or grandparents who bought stocks, precious metals, or crypto currencies for them years ago, and then forgot they had them. I know a guy who bought a bunch of Bitcoin when it first came out in 2008 as a speculation investment for a few hundred dollars. He was putting it away for his grandkids, just in case it became something in the future. As I write this book at the end of 2020, Bitcoin is at almost $20,000 a coin! Not knowing you had a handful of those around with your name on it, could definitely be helpful towards buying a home or two! Quick update: it's February 24th 2021, and I'm still working on this book. Bitcoins price today is now $49,117.31 as I write this. Quite a change in just a few short months, huh? I only bring all this up, because I want to get your creative wheels turning on different ways you can come up with cash. The old saying still stands that "cash is king." The main reason it's king is because cash puts you in a position where you don't have to borrow money to get something. If you have the cash, then you call the shots.

What's your why?

What kind of market are we in?

What's your monthly income?

What are your monthly expenses? (Rent, utilities, phone, food, gas, ect.)

Any toys? Boats, RV's, or extra vehicles?
How much do you pay for them? What is there value?

Any investments? Savings, stocks, gold, silver, crypto currencies? Inheritance or college fund?

What To Do When You Don't Have Enough

At this point you should know about how much cash you have on hand or can come up with. Now what do you do? Just for the heck of it, let's make up a scenario that you have $10,000 or less that you can come up with. That being the hypothetical case, there is a very strong chance you can't buy a livable home in the United States for cash. If you think otherwise, you are free to go on the internet and scroll homes for sale at this moment to verify. If you just went on your phone to look for homes, yet ended up scrolling your social media for awhile, then welcome back! We were talking about having $10,000 or less, and not being able buy a livable house cash for that price. Looks like you're all out of options for buying a home with cash then, huh? Not quite... we still have a few more avenues to explore.

The Gift

Do you have a relative, or close friend who will gift you the cash to buy a house? You have permission to go back on social media and look through your friends list now if you need to. If you just laughed and said, "Yeah, right, I don't have any friends or relatives that will do that," don't worry, you're not alone. Most people don't. Maybe you have a relative who will "loan", you the cash? If so, how much will they loan you?

The Cash Loan

If it is a loan, then there are some automatic questions you will need to answer. When do they want to be paid back all of the cash they loaned you? Do they want monthly payments? If so, how much do they want a month? Can you "comfortably", afford that monthly payment and pay all your other bills? Maybe you can only comfortably afford $750 a month for a house or rent payment. If you have an agreement that works on all of those questions, then you got your financing figured out, and you can go back to scrolling for homes for sale. Actually go ahead and skip all the way ahead to the purchase process chapter, and we will go from there.

Once again, if you are like most of us who have been new or first time buyers, then you don't have a relative who will loan you the cash to buy a home. Okay, so you ruled out having enough cash yourself, and can't get a gift or cash-loan. Now you're finally out of options right? I say, nay! We have one more creative option a lot of buyers don't think or know much about. It's called "seller financing!"

The Seller Financing Option

Also called owner finance, or owner carryback, depending on where you live. I'll call it seller financing, because it's more self explanatory... although I'm about to explain it to you in detail.

Seller finance, is when the seller owns the home they are selling, usually free and clear, meaning they do not owe any money on the home to any person or to any bank. This type of situation makes it possible for you to make a deal with the seller. I'll walk you through an example situation, and leave you a chart of how you can draw this type of deal up on a napkin if you ever needed to.

"Why a napkin?" you might be saying. Well, because like any good sales pitch, you probably took this seller out for something to eat, so you could talk about your idea. You didn't want to bring your notebook because that would look too obvious that you had some idea up your sleeve. Instead, you casually brought it up, and then used the waiter's pen while you were paying the dinner bill. You grabbed an extra "unused napkin," (yes unused, please don't use the one with face slobber all over it) then you wrote out the following type of scenario with the price you just talked about with the seller.

They would like to sell their home for $100,000, and you

would like to buy it for that. You will give the seller your $10,000 cash as a down payment at the closing of the sale. You now owe the sellers $90,000 as a remaining balance. You found out from the conversation over dinner that they would like to be paid off within 10 years. You already did the math on what that would cost you for a monthly payment in your head. Just to be sure you did your math right, you excused yourself just after your meal to go wash your hands in the bathroom, and check for food in your teeth. While you were in there, you used the calculator on your phone and divided $90,000 by 10. Yep the math in your head was right, it equals $9,000!

Okay, you will need to pay the seller $9,000 a year for the next 10 years. Wow... that seems like a lot of money, so you divided the $9,000 by 12. Why 12? Because there are 12 months in a year, and you are making sure the monthly payment is what you can afford.

Yes, it came out to $750 a month, which you already know you can easily afford and still save money. You write those numbers down on the napkin, and pass it across the table to the seller to look at.

> Purchase Price $100,000
> Down Payment $10,000
> Loan Amount $90,000
> Term 10 years
> Monthly Payment $750

In the best case scenario the seller accepts your offer, and you skip a few chapters to the purchase process.

Maybe the seller says, "Well this looks okay, but these payments are only paying down the principal balance. If I'm taking payments for 10 years, I want to charge an interest rate on the $90,000 you owe me."

After the record scratch sound in your head stops, you say to yourself, "...what interest rate? Oh man, I should have read that later chapter in the book about understanding interest rates!"

Yes, I have a specific chapter just ahead focusing on interest rates, and what you need to know about them. This moment would be one of the perfect scenarios of why. Possibly, the seller shoots down your entire well-thought-out napkin pitch, and just says, "No." Maybe they want the entire $100,000 all at once, because they have some plans they need the money for. If that's the case, and you know you don't have the cash, then you probably need to look into the option that most buyers take: traditional bank financing. Hey, it's not the end of the world; you will probably get a lower interest rate from the banks than you would have from the seller. The bank loans just come with a few more hoops to jump through than seller financing or cash. If you're ready to find out all about the hoops, then jump on over to the next chapter, and step right up to traditional bank financing.

Creative Cash

Gift Funds

Pros	Cons
*You don't have to pay back.	*Who gifted you the money? *Will they make you feel guilty?

Cash Loan

Pros	Cons
*No bank rules *Negotiable terms	*Payment *Short term loan?

Seller Finance

Pros	Cons
*No bank rules *No bank closing costs. *Negotiable terms *No minimum credit score.	*Payments *Higher price & interest rate

Bonus Tips!

Do you have a friend or family member that happens to own their home free and clear? Maybe you can make a deal with them for seller finance?

Also, landlords sometimes own their rental homes free and clear. They have been in the business of taking payments over the years. Maybe they would be interested in owner finance? Don't be afraid to ask.

CHAPTER 3: LOANS

In this chapter we're going to look at traditional bank home loans, what steps you take to qualify for them, and how much down payment money you will need. We will also touch on a "hard money" loan, and explain the basics of that as another possible option.

It's fair to say that the majority of us don't have a few $100,000 cash just laying around to go buy a house with. For most of us when we are starting out, we need to get some kind of loan for our first home purchase. Luckily, there are a handful of loans out there to pick from. They can range from a high-interest cash loan (often called a hard money loan) all the way to your typical low or no down payment, low-interest, traditional loan you can get from the bank. We will get into the details of a "hard money" loan later in the chapter. For the first time or new buyer, the bank loan is usually the easiest way to go for financing options.

How Much Can I Get?

Finding out how much you qualify for using a bank loan can be fairly simple to start with. There are two main options most people choose from: 1) you can set up an appointment or send your information online to the bank you use, or any bank of your choice, or, 2) going with a mortgage company.

For the first option, most people start with the bank they currently have a checking or saving account open with, as this bank already has the majority of your financial information. Instead of speaking to the normal bank teller, when you deposit your paycheck. You will speak to a loan officer that works for that bank. Those are usually the people over in the little glass office on the side that you normally don't deal with when depositing your check. Depending on the type of loans your bank offers, they will be the ones you want to speak with. Most banks offer personal loans, vehicle loans, and home loans. The loan officer can handle all of those possibilities. You can use any bank or financial institution of your choice.

Another route people often use for home loans, is a mortgage company. A mortgage company is not a bank. They are a company that helps you shop through all the bank possibilities out there to find the best loan for you. They are usually called "*(insert name)* Home Loans." In Arizona, one of the big ones is Nova Home Loans, for example. When you use a mortgage company, you will speak with a mortgage broker. They do almost the same thing that a loan officer does for the bank, except the mortgage broker will shop all of the banks offering home loans, and try to line you up with the best fit. The mortgage broker gets paid if you successfully purchase a home. Their fee is typically called an, "origination fee." It is usually 1% of the loan amount and charged as a buyer closing cost at the end of the sale.

If you want to compare the approval numbers your bank gives you to the numbers the mortgage broker finds for you, that's not a bad idea. If your bank gives you the best numbers, or the mortgage broker can't find anything better out there, then you might want to possibly save the money from what a mortgage broker will charge to set up your loan and just use your bank instead. You will also end up paying a fee for the loan officer at your bank to set up the loan, so don't think you are getting out of paying a set-up fee one way or another! The fees just might be slightly less with the bank you currently use. This may not be the case, though! That's why it's good to shop around and do your research.

To save myself a lot of extra typing, and possibly confusing you, whether you decide to use a loan officer or a mortgage broker, I'm just going to call them your "lender" from this point forward. Are we good with that? Okay, perfect let's keep moving.

Your lender will determine how much you qualify for, and how low of an interest rate you can get, from looking at how much money you make compared to how much you spend. This is called your *debt to income ratio*. Remember in the last chapter where I had you figure out and write down how much your current monthly expenses are? This is where that comes into play in the bank world of getting loans. At this point your lender is going to verify those numbers, and check your *credit score*.

Your credit score is a rating system showing how reliable you are to make your payments on time. If you have late payments, or debts you have never paid that still exist out there, they are going to show on your credit report. Your credit score can be anywhere in between 300 and 850. A score of 300 is for someone who has never made reported payments on anything, like a credit card, cell phone, or electric bill. 850 is absolutely A+ perfect… a lender's dream! Banking rules and regulations are always changing, but currently most banks won't issue a home loan to anyone with a credit score below 620, at least not without that borrower paying a much larger down payment, and being charged a much higher interest rate than normal. That borrower might have great income, and very low debt, but a horrible credit score and credit report. If your credit report shows that you haven't paid bills from the past, or worse, have been sent to collections because of it, the lender has no choice but to assume you will eventually do the same thing to them with the money you borrow.

When it comes to money, this makes sense. We all have that friend in life we let borrow something that either never returned it, or when they finally did it was damaged or broken. This is basically the same idea, except you are not the lender's friend. The better credit score and report you have will help get you the lowest possible interest rate offered at that time. The lower debt you have (basically your monthly expenses or existing loans you are already obligated to pay) combined with the higher income you have, will correlate to the higher amount of money the bank will loan you for a home. "High income, high credit scores, and low debts," is the name of the game. The lower interest rate you qualify for, means the lower payment you can expect to have.

The next factor that will help the lender determine how much you can qualify for is your down payment ability. This means how much cash do you have available to use. Good thing you did your homework in the last chapter, and already know exactly how much cash you have to work with right! I'm so proud of you! Let's use our $100,000 price from the last chapter to walk through a few different loan examples.

Conventional Loans

The most common home loan is the conventional loan. Assuming your lender approves you for the $100,000 loan example. Currently a conventional loan requires a down payment from you, the borrower, anywhere from 5% to 20% of the total loan amount. I used $100,000 for easy math, so that's anywhere from $5,000 to $20,000 of your cash you would need to use for a down payment. Again depending on your credit score and debt to income ratio will also determine what kind of down payment your lender will require from you.

A conventional loan currently requires the most amount down, of all the traditional home loans. I believe the reason for this is because the conventional loan covers almost all types of home. It's always subject to change, but it covers secondary homes, rental homes, and manufactured homes. It's definitely more diverse than the most popular first time home buyer loan: Federal Housing Administration (FHA.)

> **Down Payment Tip**
>
> You have to be able to show that you have the funds available for the down payment when you get "pre-approved" with your lender. The funds are not due until the sale of the house you're buying actually closes.

Federal Housing Administration Loans

FHA, standing for federal housing administration, is a government insured loan. It's designed to help first time home buyers with more lenient requirements than a conventional loan. For example, the current down payment requirement for an FHA loan is only 3.5% down. You only need to come up with $3,500 of your own cash using our $100,000 loan example. FHA also only requires a minimum credit score of 620 at the time, which is always subject to change as well. One catch with FHA is that you can only use it to buy a *primary residence* where you are going to live. You can't buy a secondary residence, fix-up, or rental properties with it. The primary residence you buy has to be move-in-ready to pass an FHA appraisal, which is why it's geared towards first time home buyers.

Depending on what kind of market/economy we are in, FHA also works with "down payment assistance programs." If you qualify for one of these programs, then you could have your down payment paid for you, which means you could buy a house without spending one penny of your own money!

Well... that's if you can negotiate for the seller to pay your loan closing costs for you.

"Closing costs? What's that?"

Oh that's a whole other set of fees the bank charges you up-front for loaning you the money.

on't worry I'll go over all of that with you in an upcoming chapter. This is part of those "hoops", you have to jump through when getting a loan.

> **Down Payment Assistance Program Tip**
>
> Some of these programs come with a stipulation saying if you sell or move from the home within a certain amount of years, then you owe that money back! Just check with your lender on that, or from whomever you are getting the program information.

Veteran Administration Loans

Another federally insured loan that is commonly used with bank financing is a VA loan. VA, standing for veterans administration, is a specific financing option for veterans of the military only. VA has similar restrictions to FHA, as it only approves the purchase of a primary residence. The minimum credit score is nearly the same as well. No investment properties allowed, and the home has to be in pretty much move-in-ready condition. The cool thing about VA is it requires zero down payment. Once again, if you can get the seller to pay your closing costs, then you could buy a house without spending any money out of pocket. If you are a military veteran, let your lender know and they can provide you the full guidelines of what you will need for qualification.

What loan you qualify for, or what loan you would like to use, could make a difference on the type of home you want to purchase. Certain types of properties won't be eligible to qualify for the loan you are using. If you want to buy a home that's located in a floodplain, you probably won't be able to use an FHA or VA loan. A conventional loan might be your only option for something like that. You want to find out what your loan will cover and what it will not, especially if you are looking for homes in rural areas. Some rural areas have "shared well" agreements with neighbors for water, because there is no city water in that area. There are certain loan restrictions that go along with that, along with restrictions on how many homes are on the well. These rules are always subject to change, but it's something you should ask your lender about if you know you might want a home in the country rather than a subdivision. Homes that need fix-up, or foreclosed homes being sold "as is," can be great deals as they are usually a reduced price, but you probably can't get a loan on them because of the condition they are in. Those are the deals that cash buyers or investors usually pick up at a steal. Just because you don't have the cash, and you are a first time buyer doesn't mean you can't buy homes like that. It just means you need another avenue besides traditional bank financing to get it; this is why the "hard money loan" exists.

Hard Money Loans

A hard money loan, also called an investor loan, is basically a cash loan directly to you from an individual or private company. Why is it called an "investor loan?" Because it can be used to buy a property that needs a bunch of fix up, and is

> **Hard Money Loan !!WARNING!!**
>
> A hard money loan is usually not used by first time home buyers because of the risk involved!

being sold *as is*. The investor can use the hard money loan to purchase, so the investor can use their own cash for the quick fix up. By doing it this way, they don't use up all of their own cash on the purchase... leaving themselves little or nothing left to pay for all the repairs needed.

The reason it's called "hard money" is because it is cash loaned at a *very high interest rate*, usually for a short period of time. The other reason why it's usually not for first time buyers, is that the hard money lender will require at least 50% down, most of the time.

If an investor uses a hard money loan, they try to make it as quick as possible. They want to fix the place up and sell it or refinance it to a conventional as soon as they can. What makes those high interest payments worse, is they are also usually charged as interest only.

If I've just lost you on the interest part of this explanation, I plan to clear up any confusion about interest in the next chapter I designated to understand interest rates.

> **Hard Money Stress!**
>
> I can't stress enough how risky hard money can be. I've seen the most savvy investors have something go wrong, making them lose not only their own cash, but the property as well.

If you plan on using a hard money loan for your first home purchase, because you are going to fix the home up and refinance to a traditional bank loan, please make sure you do all of your homework first. Tell your lender what your plan is, and make sure there are no loan issues or timelines with that plan. Let's move onto the next chapter discussing what your interest rate is, and why you should care.

CHAPTER 4: UNDERSTANDING INTEREST RATES.

What Is The Principal Loan Amount?

The principal loan amount is the amount of money you borrowed from someone or a company.

Okay, Then What Is Interest?

One definition of interest is the amount of money **paid**, for the **use** of someone else's money.

We will use our seller finance situation from a previous

CHAPTER 4: UNDERSTANDING INTEREST RATES.

chapter to show an example of how interest comes into the equation. Let's pick up from where we left off at that dinner table offer. You just made your offer of the $100,000 purchase price with $10,000 down, promising to pay off the $90,000 remaining balance over the next 10 years. You already know that you need to pay off $9,000 per year to pay it off in 10 years exactly. You divided the $9,000 by 12 months and came up with $750 a month.

Everything looks perfect, as you wrote it on the napkin and slid it across the table to the seller. After the seller looks over the numbers, they say, "This all looks pretty good, but these payments are for the principal balance of the $90,000 only. I want to be paid interest on my money as well."

> Purchase Price $100,000
> Down Payment $10,000
> Loan Amount $90,000
> Term 10 years
> Monthly Payment $750

Instead of being a shock, and having that record scratch sound in your head of disappointment, you now understand that interest is the amount of money paid for the use of someone else's money. You might be thinking, "Hey wait a minute Josh, I'm not using the sellers money, I'm just using their property for the next 10 years until it becomes mine."

Yes, you are correct: the seller is not loaning you the $90,000 out of their bank account. They are instead, loaning you the property they could have sold for cash, hoping you will pay them back over the 10 years according to the terms of the agreement. If you decide to not hold up to your end of the bargain during those 10 years and stop paying the seller the $90,000 you owe them, the seller's only recourse is to foreclose on the property, and take it back from you. Essentially you are paying for the use of the property loan amount valued at $90,000. That right there is where and why the interest is charged.

For the record, the seller is not *required* to charge you interest. If you are making this type of deal with family or some personal situation, then you can always set it up as "principal only payments," if the seller wants to be generous. Obviously, that is not how banks set up any loan. Whether it be for vehicles, credit cards, or home loans, banks will almost always charge interest; don't forget they are ultimately in the business to make money. Regardless, bank or not, just understand almost every seller out there, who agrees to a seller finance, is going to charge some kind of interest rate... and most likely higher than what the banks charge.

Okay, back to the dinner table and your seller finance offer.

CHAPTER 4: UNDERSTANDING INTEREST RATES.   35

Let's pretend the seller won't take less than a 6% interest rate for the life of the loan. Basically you are being charged an additional 6% of the $90,000 you owe per year, or annually, which is why it's technically called an "Annual Percentage Rate" (APR). If you want to wrap your head around what's happening mathematically, then pull up your calculator on your phone.

Type in 90,000, and multiply it by 6%. You should get 5,400. Now, divide that number by 12 months.

Yep, $450 is the amount that will be going towards interest out of your payment in the first year. You might be thinking, ok so out of my payment for $750, only $300 is paying down the principal, while $450 is going towards interest. How do I still pay that off in 10 years then? Good question... What just happened to your payment once interest was added into the equation? Let me show you.

    Since the seller wants 6% interest on the $90,000 loaned, and they want to be paid off in 10 years, then that just changed your monthly payment from $750, principal only, to $999.18, principal and interest, also called (P&I). In the loan world, that is called a (PI) payment. Almost all home loan payments are made (PITI), which I will explain shortly. I want to make sure we understand this whole interest change to your payment first. Seeing the interest added in shows why your very comfortable payment of $750 just went up by more than $200 per month to $999.18. Now you have a decision to make. Either accept the higher payment and figure out a way you're going to make it happen at those numbers, or negotiate the numbers some way in your favor. This is why you should know exactly what you can comfortably afford per month before you ever get into this deal in the first place. If you can't get the numbers down to a comfortable level for you, then you have to be willing to walk away from the deal. You can't let your emotions get in the way just because you love the idea of the house. Easier said than done, I know, but you must be stoic when it comes to buying and selling.

If you want to figure out what your payments would be for different scenarios you could offer the seller, then you need to Google an "amortization calculator" on your phone or computer. It will calculate any principal, interest, and the amount of years to pay the loan for you. Here is a free amortization calculator I found from a Google search, https://www.amortization-calc.com/. If you need to stay around the $750 per month payment, then you need to change the calculations. If you keep the numbers the exact same, but you make the years 15 instead of 10, then your PI payment would be $759.47 per month. Hey sounds good we're back in the ballpark. Now all you have to do is hope the seller will agree to an extra 5 years on payments to get their money.

The seller might counter offer you and say, "If you make a

larger down payment than $10,000, that could lower your payment as well."

In that situation you would need to have a total of a $30,000 down payment to have a principal loan amount of $70,000. This would make your payment $777.14 per month. If you don't have that much for the down payment, then you obviously can't do that. Maybe you can get the seller to agree to a lower interest rate than 6%.

The point is, there are many ways you can adjust the numbers if the seller is flexible or willing to negotiate. If you only have the $10,000 down, and the seller won't budge on the 6% interest rate, then maybe the 15 year term will be your only choice if you really want the house. The example I will show you next should help your case when it comes to getting the seller to see it that way.

Total Interest

The first example I will show you is how much the seller will make over the 10 years of the original agreement. At the end of the 10 years, the seller will be all paid back the $90,000 you owe them, plus they will have made an additional $29,902.26 in interest. This means for the original purchase price you made for the $100,000, along with the $10,000 cash down payment you gave the seller, by the end of the 10 years you will have paid $119,902.26 in total principal and interest. This is the exact reason banks and sellers charge interest on the money they loan.

Now, let's look at what happens to the numbers when we change it to a 15 year term, so you can afford those payments at $759.47. Any guesses on what might happen to the grand total you end up paying, by adding an extra 5 years of payments with interest? Let's run that same scenario at the dinner table. You tell the seller you need to keep the monthly payments near $750. You then ask to make the term 15 years instead of 10. The seller complains that they aren't sure they want to wait an additional 5 years to get paid off. They don't see what's in it for them to wait that long. You then bust out your amortization calculator and show the seller what they would be making for the 10 year agreement we just went over! The seller is pleased seeing how much interest they make, and they feel like a savvy investor. You then show them the 15 year scenario, and they will make $46,704.86 in interest alone! They will make $136,704.86 total principal and interest. If they are open to the 15 year term, then that's what's in it for them!

You might be saying, "Well that's great for the seller, but not really a win for me." Financially, yes, I agree, but it comes back down to the same old drum I keep beating on. *What's your why, and what can you comfortably afford*, if you need to buy a house.

This is also an example of why cash is still king when it comes to purchasing anything versus a loan. Maybe you are now thinking, "Well, I will just stay away from seller finance sales, and just use a bank loan instead." Hold on to your hats, I'm going to show you the traditional bank financing loan example with interest next.

Bank Loans

For easy comparison, let's use the exact same purchase price, down payment, and interest rate as the previous example. This time, you are getting pre-approved through the bank for your loan. The first difference you notice is that the payment is a very low and comfortable $539.60 per month (PI). You think to yourself:

"I could buy *two* houses with this payment, compared to that seller finance deal I almost made at the dinner table... Oh, wait, that's because the bank offers a *30 year* term to pay the loan back. Wow, that will take half of my adult life... but hey, whatever. The payment works, and I gotta live somewhere, right?"

Just for fun you pull that amortization calculator out, and punch the numbers in. Why not? You know how to figure how much interest you pay over the life of the loan, now.

$90,000 loan amount

6% interest

30 year term

You notice everything goes black because your eyes just literally popped out of your head! After you feel around the table, find your eyeballs and pop them in, you look at the screen again to make sure you read that correctly the first time. By the end of the term, you will have paid $104,251.36 *in just interest alone!* You will have paid $194,251.36 in total (PI). By the end of the term you ended up paying double for the house. Wow, you were right! You actually could have bought two homes! This again is the exact example of why I stress the idea of coming up with as much cash as you possibly can. You must clearly know the answer to *what's your why*, when it comes to possibly the biggest financial decision of your life. I don't mean to discourage you from home ownership. Real estate has and continues to make many people rich, and helped give them financial independence. You must go into it with your eyes back in your head and wide open by financially educating yourself on the numbers.

PITI

While we're on bank loans I have a few other numbers I want to go over with you that will have to do with your payment. Your home loan payment is often described as being (PITI). You now know that the PI stands for principal and interest. Can you guess what TI stands for?

Yep, you guessed it, "Taxes and Insurance." I will explain to you why these are added on as part of your monthly payment and why.

Have you ever heard the saying, "there are two certainties in life: death and taxes"? That was a quote from back in 1789 by Benjamin Franklin, and still stands to this day. Every piece of real estate in the United States is assessed at a certain amount of property taxes every year. In Arizona, the property tax bill comes out twice a year. One bill is for the first half of the year, and one bill is for the second half. If you don't pay your property taxes, then after a certain amount of time your local county can foreclose on you and take your property. Well... they can't physically remove the piece of earth titled as your property. They can just physically remove you from the property, by the power of the police. Even if you own your home free and clear, and do not owe the bank a penny, you still have to pay your annual property taxes. This is why your home loan payment includes taxes as part of your PITI payment.

You might be wondering, "How does the lender work the property taxes into my payment." I'll give you a quick example with the same purchase price and payment we were using from the bank loan example. Your current PI payment is $539.60 per month. The property taxes are $1200 a year for the home you're buying. You just divide that number by 12 months per year, and add that to your payment. Your payment is now $639.60 per month after adding $100 per month for property taxes. Now, let's look at insurance.

Insurance

Insurance is not required by law on your house... at the moment. If you own your home free and clear, you do not have to carry hazard insurance. However, without insurance, it could just be very risky if something were to happen to your home or on your property. Homeowners insurance is also called hazard insurance. It was put in place for life's little "what if's" and whoopsies.

For example, "What if a water line breaks when we're not home and floods the house ruining the floors, walls, and we get mold in our house."

Here's another possible scenario: "Wow, look at all the smoke and fire trucks on our street as we're getting home! I wonder whose house caught on fire? Whoopsie, I think I left the oven on?"

Hazard insurance is set up and paid by you to cover these types of potential losses. While you do not legally have to pay for hazard insurance if you own your home free and clear, *all lenders require* that you have insurance in place to cover at least the amount of money they loaned you if something should happen. In this way, the insurance company can pay the lender back the money they are owed if the house happens to get destroyed.

You might be wondering, "How does insurance get added to my monthly payment?" Similar to taxes, there is an annual charge to insure your home. Lets say it's $800 a year to insure the home you're buying to cover the loan amount at least. Just take $800 and divide it by 12, and you get $66. Now, add that to your payment and you have a $706.26 total PITI monthly payment.

What do you do if you decide to get pre-approved through a bank for a home loan?

First, find out how much they will approve you for, and what your PI payment would be off of that number.

Next, when you go look at homes for sale that you might be interested in, look up what the annual property taxes are. If you don't know how to find that, then look up what county the home your buying is located in. Google that county tax assessors website. Then enter the property address of the home you are buying. The property taxes are public information for you to see. Now that you know the annual property taxes for that address. Divide that number by 12, and add it to your PI payment that you already have in mind.

You also will want to contact your insurance company, and tell them how much you are pre-approved for, and get a basic quote of how much they will charge annually for a house at that price.

If you are reading this book, then you are obviously already the type of person who does their homework in life. It's almost needless to say, but I'll say it anyways: It's well worth it to do your financial education homework before you get sucked into the financial hamster wheel of payments you can't comfortably afford. At the end of the day, you want a happy home that you love, not an anxiety nest you have to live as a wage slave to pay for because someone told you it's the American Dream!

CHAPTER 5:

CLOSING COSTS

When you purchase a home, there are a certain amount of "closing costs" that go along with closing the sale. Both the buyer and the seller have their own set of closing costs applied to their side of the sale. Most of the buyer's closing costs are two sets of fee's combined together making one lump sum. The largest amount of fees have to do with your loan from the bank. The smaller set of fee's are from the title company/escrow company who handles the closing and recording of your sale. I will break down the basic fees that go along with both, as well as *why* they apply, over the next few pages. Let's start with your loan closing costs first.

Loan Closing Costs

To be clear, your loan closing costs are not your down

payment. Loan closing costs are a list of itemized fees that go along with setting up your loan from beginning to end. For the most part, you don't pay any of your loan closing costs until the day you are signing your closing documents to officially close the sale of the house. Closing costs can vary depending on the loan amount, but a good ballpark estimate is anywhere between 3% and 5% of the loan amount. Using our $100,000 purchase price example, that's $3,000 to $5,000 cash you will need, on top of your down payment money. You might be thinking, "Man, that's a lot of money." Yes, you're right! That's why a home purchase is considered one of the biggest purchases of a person's life. All the more reason to be as financially educated as you can before going into it.

What are these closing costs and why do you have to pay them? If you're using any of the traditional bank financing we talked about in a previous chapter, then you will have a certain amount of lender charges that go along with your loan. Remember the PITI payment from the last chapter? When your payment is first set up, a certain amount of taxes and insurance are impounded upfront by your lender as a closing cost. Let's use the example from the last chapter of your property taxes being $1200 a year for the home you are buying. Most lenders will want to impound at least one year's worth of property taxes when you buy the home. Many lenders will charge 18 months worth of taxes, but we will stick with 12 months for this example. Right there is your first closing cost charge of $1200. This same principle applies to your hazard insurance. Remember that $800 charge from the last chapter? Go ahead and add that on top of your $1200; you're already up to $2,000!

Now, you may qualify for the $100,000 bank loan, but before your lender loans any of that money out, they want to make sure the home is worth the price. They're not going to loan you $100,000 for a home that's only worth $50,000. Actually, they won't loan you one penny less than the actual current value of the home. Do you know how they know how much the home is really worth? If you said they pay for an appraisal you would be half right. The complete answer is that *you* pay for the appraisal. Then the appraiser can make sure the home is worth the price to the lender that loans you the money. The appraisal fee is typically anywhere between $300 and $600 on average. The only difference with this closing cost, is that you write a check and pay for this upfront during the sale. That way if the sale doesn't go through for any reason after the appraisal is complete. The appraiser still gets paid for the job they completed. What are we up to on closing costs now, about $2,500 total? It's adding up fast; let's move to the next one.

Before we go any further, most of these closing costs should not be a surprise to you at this point. When first getting approved for the loan with your lender, they will provide you with a GFE of your total loan costs. A GFE stands for "Good Faith Estimate." This is a breakdown of your itemized closing costs you can expect, and your down payment. Your lender does a lot of work to set up your loan approval, and all of your loan documents all the way until you close the sale on your new home. This is why there is a closing cost for them to get paid as well. This fee can vary, but it's typically about 1% of the loan amount paid at the closing of the sale. If your sale does not go through, the lender does not get paid... so you can bet they are doing everything they can to help you get your loan! 1% of our $90,000 loan amount gives you $900 to add in, which brings us to $3,400 in total closing costs up to this point. There might be a few other small fees you will find on your GFE, depending on what kind of loan you are using, but the ones I just went over are what you can typically expect.

A quick side note about loan closing costs: you won't have any of the lender fees for a seller finance, or a hard money loan. You will have the same title company closing costs though, which we will go over next.

Title Company Closing Costs

If you are using a title company to handle the closing of your sale, which I highly recommend, you will have a certain amount of closing fees from them as well. These fees will apply whether you are using financing or paying cash. The reason I highly recommend using a title company is because of the important role they play in the sales process. The title company's job is to research the history of the home title, called the "chain of title," as it has changed owners throughout the years since the property came of record. They make sure there are no other owners or lien holders on the title or deed of the property when it transfers from the seller to you as the new buyer. Nobody wants to buy a home they worked so hard to get, just to have some random stranger knock on the door one day saying they are part owner. This is why a typical closing cost for the seller to pay is the "title insurance." This is to insure a clear title to you as the buyer that all loans have been paid off, all property taxes are paid up to date, and no other person is on your new title as owner. The other good news is when it comes to the title company, the buyer doesn't really have much to pay in closing cost. The buyer usually splits the escrow fee and the county recorder fee with the seller. The escrow fee is usually only a few hundred dollars depending on how high the sales price is. The escrow fee is how the escrow/title company gets paid for their work. The recording fee is what your local county charges to record the sale documents and show it has officially changed hands. In most cases this fee is less than $100 dollars. Most of the buyer's big fees have to do with obtaining a home loan through the bank.

Closing Cost Help

One last tip about closing costs you are going to want to know about. Almost all loans and sales allow for you to ask the seller to pay for your closing costs... or at least a percentage of the sales price towards your closing costs, depending on what kind of loan you are using.

If you are using a conventional loan, you can ask the seller to pay *up to 3% of the purchase price* toward your closing costs. On FHA and VA loans you can ask *as much as 6%* towards your closing costs. These numbers are always subject to change with the banks making the rules. Using our purchase price example, that is $3,000 to $6,000 cash that you wouldn't have to spend out of your own pocket. Just keep in mind, the seller can always decline paying the buyer's closing costs entirely. Also understand, when you ask the seller to pay any amount towards your closing costs, it's just like asking the seller to lower the sales price by that amount. Using our $100,000 purchase price example, if you ask for 3%, or $3,000 towards your closing costs on a full price offer, then you're really only offering the seller $97,000 for the house.

If the market is a hot seller's market, where the seller is getting multiple offers for their house they usually will be inclined to hold out for a full price offer, or even a cash offer, before they will consider your offer where they are to pay closing cost.

Yet, on the other hand, when it's a buyers market, and the sellers are having a hard time selling their homes, that is a perfect time to negotiate for whatever you as the buyer would like, because you will have plenty of options to choose from. That reminds me of something I heard in a previous chapter in this book: something about what kind of market/economy we are currently in? All joking aside, knowing that information makes a big difference on how you can negotiate the numbers on your sale. Speaking of your sale, it looks like you're all approved! You've done your homework and are ready to go house hunting. I'll meet you over in the next chapter so we can start the purchase process.

CHAPTER 6: THE PURCHASE PROCESS

We all know how easy it is to look at homes for sale on the internet. You can find everything from the asking price to the price of the annual property taxes. The different sites make it easy to save particular properties you want to go look at, or at least know more about. I encourage you to do this research on your own at first, so you know what you are interested in, and why. Plus, if you want to drive by the homes on your list to check out the neighborhood and the commute, this will help you narrow things down. Once you have an idea of the homes you want to see the most, then you have some decisions to make for how to go about that.

If you already have a realtor in mind that you are going to use, then you just contact them and set up the showings. If you don't already have a realtor in mind that you are going to use, then you have a few options to pick from. You can decide to contact the agent who has the home for sale you are interested in, and set up a time for them to show you the house. Some buyers prefer to go this route, because that listing agent works directly with the seller, and has a direct line of communication. This could possibly turn into a tedious process, as you will need to contact each agent individually for the different houses you want to see. The other issue about these agents, and why they have a direct contact line to the seller, is because they have been hired by the seller to sell their home. Those agents are the sellers agents, also called the listing agents. They have a written listing agreement with the seller to represent the sellers best interest by trying to sell their house for the highest and best price they can get. The listing agent works for a commission and they get paid when the house sells; the higher the house sells for, the higher commission the listing agent makes. If the listing agent happens to write the offer for the buyer on the house they are selling, then they double their commission!

You might be saying to yourself, "Well good, they will be motivated to help me buy the house then." Yes, that's true. They'd love to have you buy the house, but remember, they have a contract with the seller to represent them and their best interest. When it comes down to negotiations, do you expect them to help you play hardball for the best deal? As a first time buyer, or a buyer who doesn't buy houses all the time, I would feel more comfortable knowing I have an agent representing my best interest.

Buyers Agents

I would recommend having a buyer's agent that is competent and has your best interest in mind, based off of what you are wanting. If you don't already have a realtor acting as a buyer's agent for you, and don't know where to find a good one, call a few of the realtors that have multiple homes for sale in the area you like, and tell them what you are looking for. After a 20 minute phone conversation with them, you should have a pretty good idea of how knowledgeable they are of the area and current market. After they find out you are all pre qualified and have done your homework, they will probably jump at the opportunity to help find you a home. If they happen to be too busy, they probably know of another realtor to whom they can refer you.

Besides looking out for your best interest, and helping you negotiate your offer, one of the best parts about having a buyer's agent, is you usually don't have to pay them. *You mean they work for free?* No, they don't work for free. They receive a "co-op fee" offered from the listing agent that has the home for sale. For example, the listing agent charges the seller a 6% commission fee to sell their house. The listing agent then offers 3% to any agent who brings a ready, willing, and able buyer to purchase the home. That 3% co-op fee is what your buyer's agent gets paid if you buy the house, so you don't have to pay them any money out of pocket. It's a pretty good deal for the buyer. You have a realtor who has no connection to the seller, they represent you exclusively, and you don't have to pay them out of your own pocket.

When you find a buyer's agent you are going to use, and are ready to go look at houses, make sure you tell the agent what price you want to stay at or stay below. Tell them you only want to look at homes that can be purchased in the price point you want to stay in. All of this is of course assuming you have your down payment and closing costs money set aside for the purchase price you are figuring on. Let me give you an extra suggestion before you go looking at any houses you might want to buy. Just in case your buyers agent forgets to tell you, I'm telling you now. Plan to have an extra $1,000 of spending money ready for when you find the home you want to buy. You will need it when your offer gets accepted.

You're probably thinking, "Oh man, more money?" Unfortunately, yes. But, it's for a reason that is well worth it! When you get your offer accepted by the seller for the home you want to purchase, your due diligence/inspection period starts the first day after contract acceptance. In the Arizona contract, you have a 10 day period pre printed into the contract language for you to hire any inspectors you feel necessary. Notice the word, "hire", in the last sentence. It's highly recommended that you hire a licensed home inspector and a pest inspector during this 10 day period. I will get into the details of why, very soon, but the point is that those inspectors will cost a few hundred dollars. Having that in mind, and in your bank account, is a good idea before you go looking at houses, so you're not scrambling from the start. With that being said, now I think you are completely prepared to make a legitimate offer on a house you like. Let's get your offer accepted.

> **Bonus Tip!**
>
> Plan to have an extra $1,000 of spending money ready for when you find the home you want to buy. You will need it when your offer gets accepted.

Offer Acceptance

What kind of market you are currently in will determine how the negotiations will go on your offer. There are countless scenarios of offers and counter offers we can make up. To keep things simple, let's say your offer has been accepted at a price you are happy with. Since we made up a scenario let's make up some dates to go with it. Your offer is accepted on November 1st, and you have an agreed upon closing date of December 1st. This is basically a 30 day escrow period. Actually, a little less when you take away weekends and that long Thanksgiving day weekend when banks and title companies are closed. Your purchase contract is calculated by calendar days, not business days. However, you must take into account business days, because certain players in the game, like your lender and the title company, will not be open on all days. This is the normal part of the sale process for anyone, so just roll with it. The good news is, your offer is officially accepted, and you are moving forward with the deal. What happens now?

The First Steps

To start with, your buyer's agent takes your accepted contract, along with your earnest money check, to the title company to open escrow.

"Earnest money what's that?"

In short, it's similar to a deposit that is assigned to the title company when your offer is accepted. It's basically an act of good faith showing your earnest intent to buy the home. Your earnest money can be some of your down payment or closing cost money you have saved, and can be applied to either one when your sale closes on December 1st. Earnest money can be any amount you want to offer. I've seen it anywhere from hundreds of dollars to thousands. This is the generally accepted rule of earnest money: the higher it is, the more serious of a buyer the seller understands you to be.

"Why is that?" you might be asking.

For example, if you went all the way through the sale to the last week of November, and suddenly changed your mind about buying the house and backed out of the deal, the seller can't force you to buy the house. However, as recourse, the seller could be entitled to keep your earnest money as per contract. Most people aren't planning on just walking away from a few thousand dollars. This is why earnest money becomes an important part of the purchase worth mentioning.

SPDS

As I mentioned, your due diligence/inspection period begins the day following contract acceptance as well. You should also be provided with any seller disclosure forms within the first 5 days of contract acceptance. In Arizona most sellers will have filled out an SPDS, standing for, "Seller Property Disclosure Statement." This form has over 200 yes/no questions that the seller has answered regarding anything they know about the home. This might be called something different in other states, but it should still cover the same topics of seller disclosure.

This disclosure statement covers almost every part of the home including but not limited to: plumbing, electrical, roofing, pest issues, termites, environmental issues, additions built onto the home without permits, ect.

The seller has to answer every question with a yes, no, or additional explanation of anything they are aware of. You, as the buyer, will have to initial the bottom of every page, sign, and date the last page as acknowledgment. This form will help you learn about the house you intend to own, and is great information to share with your home inspector if you choose to hire one.

Inspection Period

At this point, in addition to having a signed contract and escrow being opened, your due diligence/inspection period begins. In most contracts, you have a 10 day period to inspect for basically anything you want.

If you or someone you know happen to know your way around all the functions of a home, then you are of course free to conduct your own home inspections. Depending on what type of home loan you are using, your lender might require you to hire a licensed home inspector. FHA has a form your lender will make you sign titled, "for your protection get a home inspection." In that case, a home inspection is an absolute requiremnet for the loan. Keep in mind, loan rules and regulations are always subject to change anytime the banks want to change them. FHA and VA have been requiring pest inspections, mainly termite inspections, in Arizona for years. I can't say I blame them for this either. If I were loaning out hundreds of thousands of dollars for homes, I'd like to know they are in good condition as well.

Home Inspectors

If your lender does *not* require that you hire a home inspector, and you choose to conduct your own home inspection, any good realtor will have you sign your life away that you have been warned to hire professional inspectors. Your realtor's job is to look out for your best interest, but they also need to look out for themselves. If your realtor is not sharp enough to cover their own assets, they probably aren't sharp enough to cover yours. No matter how savvy of a buyer you are, it's always good to get the opinion of a licensed professional who inspects homes for a living. This is where having that extra $1,000 will come in handy. Depending on the square footage of the house you're buying, plus any outbuildings like garages or guest homes, the cost of a home inspection can be anywhere between $300 and $600 at the time I write this book (April 2021). A termite inspection takes less time, and is usually between $50 and $100 at this time as well. Having that extra $1,000 should help you easily pay for these inspections, as well as any extra fees, should the inspectors recommend another professional to look at something in more detail. For example, a home inspector might be able to point out that an A/C or a furnace is not blowing at the proper temperature; however, they may not be able to point out exactly why it isn't working. In this case, they might recommend that you have a licensed HVAC technician look at the system.

You might be thinking, "Wow, this is turning into a lot of money just to have a home inspected."

I agree! It does, but think of it this way. A home inspector finding a costly defect, like faulty electrical wires that could cause a fire, leaking plumbing, roofing, or a list of any other major issues, could save you thousands of dollars, *or even your life*, from discovering them too late once you own the home. The same can be said for a termite inspector possibly finding that the frame and roof of your home is on the verge of collapse from years of untreated termite infestations. These, along with a list of other possible home issues, you need to know upfront. Find out *before* committing to a $100,000 home loan, and 30 years of payments. When you look at it that way, a few hundred dollars for professional inspections isn't too bad.

Your realtor can help you schedule the inspectors to check the home out during your inspections period. I would recommend being present for the home inspection day. If you can't be present the whole time, as the home inspector usually takes about three hours on the typical home, then at least try to be there by the end. This is when the inspector goes over their findings. When the home inspector completes the inspection, they will usually have a 30+ page report to print out or email to you. They will go over every item in the house they inspected for, and usually have detailed digital pictures of any repair item(s) they discovered. Have you ever heard the saying, "A picture is worth a thousand words?" This is definitely the case when you're trying to explain exposed electrical wires in the attic where nobody usually goes. Clear digital pictures is all you need to negotiate that repair with the seller.

Termite/Pest Inspector

The termite/pest inspector has a process very similar to the home inspector. They also provide a written report with a map of the house's floor plan, showing any areas they found evidence of past or present pest infestations.

I don't care how well you or your friend, know your way around home repairs. If you don't know how to spot pest problems, you could be asking for major problems. I know of a story that sounds like it's right out of a horror movie.

A couple bought a new house in a brand new subdivision, that had just been built. They figured since the house was brand new, there couldn't be anything wrong with it. So, they waived any inspections. After moving in, they started noticing scorpions all over the house. After finally having a scorpion drop from the ceiling onto the poor woman's head, they called a pest inspector who discovered a nest of scorpions in the walls of the home. The pest inspector removed the nest, and treated the entire home for scorpions with the understanding that it may take a few weeks before they are all gone. Needless to say, that led to some sleepless nights before the couple could finally get comfortable in their new home. I can't emphasize enough: take advantage of your inspection period!

Inspections (Continued)

By this point, you should have your inspection reports in hand, or at least saved on your computer. Hold onto them. You are going to need them by the end of your inspection period. Before that time comes, I want to point out a few other things to think about looking into, that the home inspector *can't* help with.

How about looking into some of the neighborhood factors for the home you're buying? This internet age we live in makes it so easy to find out anything... from the crime rate, to sex offenders in the vicintity.

How about planes, trains, and automobiles? Meaning, how much traffic noise will you get? If you found out a train comes through blasting its horn everyday at certain times, would you be ok with that? Will you live next door to the guy who cranks up his hotrod car every night, or the garage rock band practicing until dawn?

How about your commute to work, and the traffic that goes with it? Obviously every person is different with different needs and concerns. My point is to make sure you think outside the box for the moment. You might be able to ask the seller to fix the dripping sink, but they can't do much about the airport noise. Find out what you can during your inspection period, so if there is something you absolutely cannot live with, you can cancel the sale and move on.

Wrapping Up Inspections

Speaking of possibly canceling the sale, let's move onto the end of your inspection period. You have gone over all the reports with your realtor, and all of your neighborhood due diligence as you near day 10 of your inspection period. Whatever you discovered will dictate what you decide to do next. Your realtor will now provide you with another document to sign called your BINSR, standing for "Buyers Inspection Notice, and Seller's Response." The BINSR gives you three options to pick from.

Option 1

If the home is in great condition, you are happy with everything, and no major issues are discovered, then you might choose the option saying something like, "...buyers accept home in its current condition, and choose to move forward with the sale." That's the *best* case scenario that all parties hope for.

Option 2

The next option you might choose to exercise is if you find some minor issues with the home that can be repaired, or replaced. If that is the case, then you can list the items on the BINSR, along with the inspection report that refers to them, and ask that the seller repair or replace. The seller will now have a certain amount of days (usually 5 days) to respond to your request in writing. The seller can choose to accept, deny, or write a response of their own. If the seller accepts, then you will move forward with the sale with the agreement that the repairs will be completed by the closing date of the sale. If the seller denies, or gives you a written response of their own, then the ball is back in your court. You now have the choice to agree to the seller's response and move forward with the sale, or immediately cancel the contract and get your earnest money back. That also happens to be the third option to the BINSR.

Option 3

If you find something during your inspection period that you can't live with, whether the seller fixed it or not, then you are within your rights to cancel the contract without any negotiations, and receive your earnest money back.

Cancellation Option Heads Up

If you do decide to cancel the sale, and go back to house hunting, you won't get back any of the money you used to hire inspectors to do their jobs. As I said before, $300 to $600 to possibly save you thousands... or your life... is well worth it.

Hopefully all goes well, and you move forward with your sale. If that is the case, then congratulations. You just crossed one of the major hurdles in the home buying process. You are now ready to head into the last half of your sales process. I broke the second half of the process up into the next chapter to give you a chance to absorb all of this information a bit at a time. The next chapter will have to do with the "loan and title company" portions of your home purchase. If you are ready for the next step, I'll meet you over there! If you need a break, I don't blame you, but I'll still meet you over there when you're ready!

CHAPTER 7: CLOSING THE DEAL

Good news, you just cleared a major hurdle with the inspection period, and you are at least halfway through the sales process! Now you are about 2 or 3 weeks away from closing on the sale of your new home. At this point, it's easy to start getting excited, but do yourself a favor and relax. I know that's easier said than done, but we still have a few more hurdles to jump over before this race is over. These ones will have to do with your loan, and the title of the home. Some of these potential hurdles will be completely out of your hands, which is why I want you to relax. Let's start with what is out of your hands, and then finish with the items that you can completely control.

The Title Company

During your 30 day escrow period, the title company you

are using to handle the sale... you know, the same one that you made your earnest money check out to? Yes, them! They will be contacting you through phone or email to send you a "buyer information and welcome" packet. The packet will ask you for all required information that the title company needs from you to set up the title, note, and deed for your new home.

They will also explain what items the title company will insure from the preliminary title report, commonly called, "the prelim." Most people don't pay much attention to the prelim because it seems like confusing real estate jargon; it's easy to assume the title company will handle it all. The prelim is an important piece of information of which to at least understand the basics. It will show anything found on the title history that the seller needs to pay off before the property can be transferred to you at closing. If the seller has any liens or unpaid property taxes against the property, they will need to be paid out of the seller's proceeds before the title company can insure clear title to you as the new owner.

The title company will also look through the history of the title, also called the "chain of title." They look as far as the title goes back in history, to make sure there are no other owners attached to the title of the home. As I touched on in a previous chapter, the last thing you or anybody wants is to be moved into your new home, and have someone knock on the door informing you that they are partial owners as well. That example is why the seller pays for title insurance to transfer clear title to the buyer at close of escrow. If the title company finds any issues, or "clouds," as they call it, on the title, they will notify all parties immediately.

An example of a possible issue would be the heirs of a deceased person selling the home. The home is still in the name of the deceased person, so to insure clear title, the title company would need proper documentations, such as probate orders from the court, a will, or death certificate, before they could let the sale proceed. If for some reason any of the proper documentation couldn't be provided, or was still held up in court, the sales closing date would be extended until the issue was cleared up. If the issue could not be cleared in a timely manner for you as the buyer, then you can choose to cancel the sale. Most people, along with some realtors might feel that since it's the title company's job to take care of these types of issues, then you don't really need to pay attention to the prelim.

I don't assume that to be true, because the title company will also have a page with a list of items they will *not* insure on the prelim. These are the items you want to pay attention to and go over with your realtor. A common example of something the title company will not insure is easements. For most people purchasing a home in a subdivision, this probably won't be much of an issue. For people who are purchasing in rural areas, or out in the country, easements are worth paying attention to. An easement is usually a public or private right of way that is somehow connected with your property. Utilities for electric or water, leading from the main line source to your house, are a common example of an easement. Usually, you can't fence off or block these right of ways, because the utility companies will need access to them if ever needed. Utility easements are common with many sales, and usually not an issue.

Public or private use pathways can be another story. If you have any legal easements for ingress or egress across your property, by anyone other than yourself, you want to know about it before you purchase. The only way you will know is by looking over the page of exceptions on the prelim and finding out. Your sales contract should have a provision about the prelim giving you a certain amount of days to disapprove of any items you find. Take advantage of asking for the details of any information you find on the "Exceptions" page of the prelim. Most of the time, everything checks out just fine, and you can comfortably clear that small hurdle to move forward with the sale.

The Appraisal

Usually, the same time as the prelim is happening, your

lender will start the appraisal order for the home. This is the point where your lender will ask you to write out a check for around $400 to $600, made out to the appraisal company. Since the buyer's lender is the one who requires an appraisal of the home, then the buyer is usually the one who pays for it. The appraiser's job is to go out to the home, or the "subject property," as the appraiser calls it, and view the home inside and out. The appraiser will take many pictures of what they find, measure, and compare. I will not go into covering all of the complex detailed research an appraiser does, as it would be an entire book by itself, and *I am not an appraiser*. I will, however, give you a basic summary of what they do, and point out how that affects your home purchase.

An appraiser will compare the subject property with usually at least three comparable properties sold within a similar time frame. They basically have a painstakingly detailed process to assure the sales price is accurate with the current market conditions. What that means for *you* as the buyer, and for your lender, is that the property is worth the price you are paying for it, and what your lender is loaning on it. Although the appraiser is not a home inspector, they will take pictures and notes of any adverse conditions they find with the home or property.

A common example is the roof of the subject property. If the appraiser notices missing shingles or roof tiles, they will take pictures and notes of it in the appraisal report. Then, when the appraisal is completed, the full report and pictures go to the loan underwriter to look over. The appraisal price might come in just perfect right at the sales price, but it might be under the condition that the roof be repaired. Usually, it will say something to the effect that a, "...licensed roofer must inspect the roof, and insure the life of the roof," for a certain amount of time the lender asks for. Once something like this happens, everything is out of your hands. If the roofer decides a whole new roof needs to be put on the home, then the lender will require that work to be completed before they will loan the money for the sale. In most cases, a new roof is thousands of dollars that someone will need to come up with before the sale can move forward. In the buyer's position, you will of course want the seller to pay for it. The seller will be thinking, "Hey, I won't be living here in the future... *you will!* So why don't you pay for it?"

If neither party will pay for a new roof or come to some kind of agreement, then the lender will not loan the money on the house, and the sale will be dead. What that means for you as the buyer is a return of your earnest money, and it's back to house hunting. What it means to the seller is that they are back on the market as well, but with a new disclosure to add to the SPDS. The seller will now have the task of selling their home with a report from a licensed roofer saying the roof needs to be replaced. They will possibly need to come down on price to compensate, so a buyer can afford to assume the responsibility, or sell to a cash buyer as is that will assume the responsibility. Hopefully when the seller understands those options, they will be negotiable with you to find a reasonable solution. This is another example of why I say not to get too excited about your new home yet. The appraisal can sometimes point out issues you might not be able or willing to move forward with.

This is where having a good realtor becomes so valuable during the sales process. They can potentially see pitfalls like these coming, especially if these items were pointed out during your inspection period. A good realtor will most likely know what home inspection issues will also be loan and appraisal issues. Missing shingles you can possibly see from the ground, should be a no-brainer to a seasoned realtor. If the items were noted and photographed during the home inspection, then they shouldn't be a surprise to you or the seller either. That is another reason I believe the home inspection is well worth the money.

Majority of the time, all goes well with an appraisal of a home in good condition at a fair market price. If that is the case for you, then congratulations; you just cleared one of the last big hurdles and the sale is moving forward. By this point you are probably one or two weeks away from owning your new home. Can you start to get excited yet? I say nay! Save that excitement energy for unpacking all those boxes when you move in.

Finalizing The Loan

At this point your lender will probably be contacting you with updates about your loan status. They might ask for more documentation like pay stubs from your employment check, updated bank statements, and run your credit again. This part right here is where a first time buyer can slip up. The reason the lender is running all of your information again, is to make sure nothing has negatively changed since they first pre-approved you for the loan weeks ago... or sometimes months ago. The lender is verifying you are still employed, and making the same amount of money or more. They want to make sure you still have your down payment and closing cost money in your bank account.

They also want to run your credit again to make sure your score hasn't dropped, or your debt to income ratio hasn't changed. Please hold off making any purchases on credit until your house sale officially closes escrow. Any negative change to

!WARNING!
If you are just dying to go buy that new living room set on your credit card that will go perfectly in your new home, DON'T!

your debt to income ratio, or credit score can severely affect the approval of your home loan. I've heard of people's sales completely falling apart because a drop in their credit score disqualifies them for the loan and interest rate they were approved for.

Final Walkthrough

> **BONUS TIP!**
> Before you go buy anything for the house, have a move-in party when the sale closes. Let friends and family come see all the things you need for your new home!!

Besides the thought of possible housewarming gifts, the good news is that you are almost to the final closing date you've been waiting on. At this point, everything is pretty much out of your hands. Your lender will be finalizing all of your loan documents, and the title company will be setting up all of their documents for you to sign. All you have to do is not put anything on credit, or spend any of your down payment and closing cost money. Within a week or less of the closing date, your realtor should contact you to set up your final walkthrough of the house. This is your chance to look at the home one more time, and make sure it's in the same condition as when you made the offer. At this point the seller should be all moved out; the home should be empty and hopefully clean. Sometimes, during the seller's move out process the home can get damaged. If you find damages, then your final walkthrough is the time to point that out. The same goes for any repairs the seller has agreed to do from your inspection requests. If the seller agreed to repair the leaking kitchen faucet, then go check the faucet and make sure! If you find anything that is in worse condition, or items that have not been repaired, your realtor will have a final walkthrough form for you to sign and list any disapproved items you find.

Your realtor will now deliver this form to the seller or sellers realtor immediately. At this point neither party wants the sale to be extended or delayed over a minor issue, so usually the seller will remedy what's needed right away. The moving process can take its toll on the seller, so try to be understanding if they forget a thing or two. Hopefully your final walkthrough goes great. Most of the time they do. If that is the case, then you are ready to set up a signing time and day with the title company and move forward.

Review Your Settlement Statement

By this point, you are just a couple days away from your signing day. The title company will send you, your realtor, and your lender a copy of the final settlement statement for approval.

The settlement statement is an itemized list of the funds

you will need to bring to the signing in the form of a certified bank check or wired funds. The itemized fees are a combination of your closing costs, along with your down payment, added up to one whole number. This number should not be a surprise to

> **!WARNING!**
> Cash is not accepted by the title company at close of escrow. Do not show up to close of escrow with a suitcase full of cash.

you, as it should be very close to your GFE number from a previous chapter. That's the "Good Faith Estimate" you got from your lender when you first got pre-approved for your home loan. They call it a Good Faith *Estimate*, because it should be very close to your actual final settlement statement fees. The fees wont be exact because of different property tax prices of homes, insurance rates, and what you have negotiated with the seller in the contract. The numbers should be very close though, and definitely should not be a shock from what you were expecting. If there are any fees you don't understand, now is your chance to bring it up for clarification. Every now and then people make typos, or put fees from one side to the other, not knowing it was negotiated in the contract. Don't get all bent out of shape if that happens, just calmly point it out, and have your documentation to go along with it.

Signing Day

If all the fees look like what you were expecting on the final settlement statement, then on your signing day and time, take your funds down to the title company to close the sale. Oh, and don't forget your ID, as the title officer will need to notarize your signature.

At the title company, you will have a stack of loan and sale documents to sign with the title officer. They will walk you through each form as you sign, giving you a brief summary of what each one is. If you want to read the entire stack word for word before you sign, then please let your realtor know, so they can inform the title officer. They will need to set aside a few extra hours for you to do this. The combinations of your loan documents along with the sale documents can be the size of this book. If you have done all of your homework up to this point, as we have in this book, then you should be just fine with the title officer's summary of each form as you sign. Once you sign all of your closing documents, and hand over your funds, then the sale is complete. Congratulations! You now own a new home... well, almost.

Once your documents are all signed, they go back to your lender to approve your signatures. Once approved, your note, and deed of trust are sent to your local county recorder's office to be officially made a public record. This process removes the seller's name from the property title and taxes. Your name is now replaced as the new owner of record. Once the documents are recorded, your lender simultaneously funds your loan, and the sale is complete.

The keys to the house now belong to you; as the new owner, I grant you permission to be officially excited! Haul those moving boxes in the door and unpack. Congratulations... you did it! The house is officially yours! Pat yourself on the back. You are now a homeowner!

Buyers Checklist

Common Documents

*Purchase Contract
*Seller Disclsoure (SPDS)
*Covenants, Conditions, and Restrictions (CC&Rs)
*Homeowner's Association Documents (HOA)
*Title Report
*Loan Info Documents
*Home Inspection Report
*Termite Inspection Report

Common Property Conditions

*Repairs & Remodeling
*Roof Condition
*Square Footage
*Sewar/Septic
*Water/Well Issues
*Fire/Flood Damage
*Pest/Rodents/Termites
*Property Boundaries
*Plumbing/Heating/Cooling
*Insurance Claims/Damage

Buyers Checklist Continued

Common Conditions Affecting The Area Surrounding The Property

*Enviromental Concerns
*Super Fund Sites
*Electromagnectic Fields
*Freeways/Traffic Conditions & Construction
*Military & Public Airports
*Planning & Zoning Information in Neighborhoods
*Schools
*National Parks & Forested Areas
*Sex Offenders
*Crime Statistic

Do your Research

-Investigate your Surroundings
-Talk to the Neighbors
-Drive Around the Neighborhoods

Resources

To find out more about Superfund sites go to.

https://www.epa.gov/superfund/what-superfund

For more about Electromagnetic fields go to.

https://www.who.int/health-topics/electromagnetic-fields#tab=tab_1

Find out more about almost any city in the United States by going to, Best Places.Net

https://www.bestplaces.net/

AFTERWORD

I never thought I would write a book. Heck, I never thought I'd ever learn to play that guitar that's been sitting in the closet the last 20 years either. There are a lot of things we seem to get the notion that we can't do, or just seem too far out of reach. Writing this book, and playing the guitar have taught me something: the more you educate yourself about something, the more confindent you will feel about doing it. The more you do it, the more experience you gain. The mistakes you make along the way don't end up really being mistakes at all. They end up being teachers, which turn into more experience, and eventually confindence.

If you read this book, then you already took a huge step towards educating yourself about the home buying process. If you still find yourself concerned with any unknown possibilites and doubts that plague our complex human minds, I urge you to take a good look at whatever that fear or concern is. Get right down to the root of it, and find out everything you can about the subject.

The knowledge you gain will truly give you power. Play it all the way through your mind like a game of chess. What will be your final move? Your exit strategy? Maybe you will want to educate yourself about how to sell your home after you buy it? If you decide to get past being a first time home buyer, then you might eventually become a first time home seller. Who knows, maybe you will find out so much, that you will become a real estate investor yourself! I have met many people over the years that are financially set for the rest of thier lives because of real estate investing. Guess what? They all started out as first time buyers at some point as well. Most of those people never went to college; some of them never even graduated from high school. Yet, at some point in their life they decided to financially educate themselves about real estate.

Your financial education might be the most important education you receive in this monetary world we live in. Don't be afraid of it. Anyone can do it in this information age that we all have at our fingertips. Speaking of fingertips, it's time for my guitar playing session. I've learned finger picking style for some of my favorite songs that I'm proud to say I can now play. I hope this book has helped you in your process of deciding if homeownership is right for you. Enjoy the ever changing process, and follow your bliss!

ABOUT THE AUTHOR

Josh Mattison

Josh Mattison joined the family real estate business as a licensed agent in 2002. He became a real estate broker and took over the business by 2005, which is also when he bought his first investment property. Josh has helped 100's of first time buyers, sellers, and investors pursue their real estate goals. During the 20 years of residential real estate sales, Josh has become a fulltime real estate investor, specializing is bank foreclosures, property flips, and residential rental property.

FIRST TIME HOME BUYING BASICS

www.ingramcontent.com/pod-product-compliance
Lightning Source LLC
Chambersburg PA
CBHW050246220526
45465CB00002B/566